Story

Journey

Spirit

Karen Gronback Johnson

To Vivian

who read to me

and

to Michael

always

Published by Human Error Publishing
www.humanerrorpublishing.com
paul@humanerrorpublishing.com

Copyright © 2020
by
Human Error Publishing
&

Karen Gronback Johnson

All Rights Reserved

ISBN#: 978-1-948521-43-7

Cover design
by
Paul Richmond and Karen Gronback Johnson

Human Error Publishing asks that no part of this publication be reproduced or transmitted in any form or by any means electronic or mechanical, including photocopy, recording or information storage or retrieval system without permission in writing from Karen Gronback Johnson and Human Error Publishing. The reasons for this are to help support publisher and the artist.

Table Of Contents

Introduction — 8
STORY — 10

Escape by Night — 11
Flying — 13
Don't Look Back   Mr. Silbermann — 15
The Past — 17
Dixwell Sestina — 18
Not My Dream — 20
Epilogue — 22
Clothesline — 23
Second Wedding — 25
Neighbors — 26
Cathrine   My Sister — 27
Fast Kenny — 28
Lansing NC 2014 — 29
About the Field — 30
Photograph, June 1, 1928 — 31
Picnic on the Hudson — 32
In Confidence — 33
Sand Yachting — 34
Lunchtime—West Haven — 35
Propositioning Carrie Ann — 37
Summer Cottage — 38
Where No Compass Guides — 39
Home Visit — 40

JOURNEY — 42

Acrophobia II — 43
Gestation — 44
Guilford Trilogy
I West River Summer — 45
II Nut Plains Autumn — 47
III Cockaponsett Winter — 49
Lost Poem — 51

Garden Journal—July 3 — 52
Anger — 53
Awake — 54
Exile — 55
Talisman — 56
On The Footbridge — 57
Challenge — 59
Impetus — 60
Nearing the Solstice — 62
Listening for Orion — 63
Reserve America — 64
Love After All — 65
Unpacking the Move — 66
Learning the House — 67
Veranda Lullaby — 68

SPIRIT — 70

Creation — 71
A Priming of Parts — 72
Drum Song — 73
Because... — 74
Parable — 75
Burial Rites — 77
Bereaved — 78
Snow will come — 79
Love Song — 80
Advent — 81
In Surrender — 82
A Winter's Tale — 84
Toward Epiphany — 86
Mandala — 87
In the Woods   God — 88
Fifteen Minutes — 89
Thanksgiving — 90
Swallowed by Sinkhole — 91
Lazarus   Afterward — 93
Legion — 94
The Mathematics of Grapes — 96
Waning Moon at Break of Day — 97

Introduction

I remember sitting in my mother's lap listening to her read nursery rhymes and other poetry to me and my brother. I remember listening to the sound of the words, though I didn't understand them all. I remember cadence and rhyme. This was different from the way people talked.

I was brought up in New Britain, CT, then a factory city with the nickname Hardware City of the World. My father worked for the city as an arborist, preferring to work outside at any cost. We went on picnics and hikes almost every weekend, to get away from the city.

In second grade I wrote a poem named "Swinging in Fairyland". I was accused of plagiarism. Did my mother read such a poem to me? Did I find it in a book? No. I wrote it. It won a contest.

I was class poet when I graduated high school.

I went to state college for a few semesters on and off, majoring in theater arts; worked in an insurance company, went to California for a year, wrote lyrics for a rock band.

When I moved to Guilford, CT, I took a class offered by poet Rebecca Newth at the Guilford Handcrafts Center. It was the beginning of what would eventually become, after many iterations, the Guilford Poets Guild. At that time and for some time after, we would meet every week to share our poetry and offer it for critique. I wrote about dreams a lot. They didn't seem to have much to do with my daily life, often including people I didn't know in circumstances foreign to me. But then, they were my dreams.

In 1995, I started graduate school at Andover Newton Theological School in Newton Centre, MA. Poetry took a back seat with school, a husband and two small children, and various church responsibilities connected to my studies. After graduation I took a few interim positions, and finally accepted a full-time call to the Old Stone Church, United Church of Christ, in East Haven, CT. In 2008 I was able to take a sabbatical, and returned to my old friends, the Guilford Poets, only to find out they were now a Guild. Some of them remembered me well enough to take me in. I think I was only one of two of them working full time.

Guilford Poets Guild collaborates with Florence Griswold Museum in Lyme, CT, and the Madison Arts Association, to write ekphrastic poetry about the art included in their various shows and installations. This is the basis for much of the poetry in the first chapter of this book, Story.

In 2016, it was time to retire. At last I could pursue my Journey toward the more rural and earth-centered living that had been calling me for most of my life, since those hikes and picnics of my childhood. After many trips tent camping in Ashe County, NC, and southwestern VA, my husband and I found a 90-year-old quasi-craftsman style brick house in Lambsburg, VA, with a huge wrap around porch and ample flat space for gardening. It sits at the base of Sugarloaf Mountain, which provides access to hiking trails replete with woods, wildlife and wild flowers.

Soon after our move, I sought out fellow writers, and though they mostly are not poets, they tolerate me and do have insightful comments and critiques. As most of these Ridgeline Writers are published, they have been encouraging me to compile some of my work.

Through much of my life I have felt that God had a home for me, and that is where I have placed my trust. I have not been disappointed. In this place, surrounded by the beauty of the Blue Ridge Mountains I have found solid friendships, and space for my Spirit to thrive.

June, 2020

STORY

Escape by Night

My directions
should get you there safely
if you leave the car
and stay off the road
While they search for you
I will pack what I dare

If I do not run
I will remember
to put out the cat
to take small things of value
and warmer clothes for you
It is time

The dog and I reach
the succoring woods
as headlights return
I make a game with her
so she will not look back
until we reach the orchard

I do not know this land
have seen it only
in aerial photographs
trees and skeletal branches
frame in rusty black
long lanes of snow

No owl hunts now
No cloud sets out to interrupt
the mindless moon
I plunge through virgin drifts
dog following in my track
more easily than forging her own

We should reach you before dawn turns
the trees to umber and mauve
before spring sets gentler snow
upon their boughs
before the hard green apples
swell and blush.

Flying

Icarus had dreams of flying
sometimes late at night   the waves soughing
nuzzling the island beach in darkness
or early   before the stars
were altogether paled into the bluing sky
before the seabirds woke to curse
and scold the boats in harbor
Sometimes in this soft time
when no breeze twitched a leaf
and all was cool and clean
he dreamed he flew

The pose was less important
than clearing the mind   ascent
and maneuver attained purely
by desire   a resolve to rise
with the mist following morning streams
until the final sun burned
across wondering hills to wake
the village   He knew
no other home

   When Dedalus awoke   his dream
   remained long enough to trick him
   and for an instant he believed
   he was in the city   waking to plan
   the day's work for his craftsmen
   and apprentices   With bitterness
   he remembered the incomplete drawings
   his temple to Apollo   He rose
   to gather duck eggs and any feathers
   that might be left on their daily path
   to the pond

And so it was that Icarus would
fly   in secrecy
in the dream time before dawn
launched from the cliffs that shadowed

the gentle beach   straining to reach
the higher winds   the carrying sky
he flew   the back of his father
laboring hard before him
behind him   all he knew
without a final good-bye   no way
to turn and stamp a memory
on his heart   his father's words
a litany in his ears

> *Your body is the craft*
> *keep your legs thus*
> *arch your back*
> *do not twist or fidget*
> *practice   practice*
> *This is the plan*

Now the day was calm and clear
the sea a thousand gemstones
          emerald   tourmaline
the sky a bolt of brilliant silk
but always the work
of flapping wings   his father
a speck in the distance
the sun hot on his back.

Don't Look Back   Mr. Silbermann

The words came clean
and sudden   in response
to a cue in some play
>*At this point   Silbermann   you cross
>downstage   pause by the rose arbor
>and continue off*

or murmured in the sterility
of the hospital or funeral parlor
by one who only means
to comfort or encourage
>*Don't look back*

or as if heard through an open
window of a summer hot apartment
the blue television flicker reflected
in a mirror   the soap opera music swelling
as Silbermann's footsteps fade

or memory of an incident too hard
for memory   the mind has blocked
but somehow cannot altogether forget
>*Please, you must take these
>documents to the Embassy
>No matter what you may hear
>or perceive to be happening
>don't look back   Mr. Silbermann*

Mr. Silbermann   why have you come
to me now as I fry bacon
for quiche with onions   mushrooms
this dark frozen January   the house quiet
and warm   the dog resting on the rug

Who are you   Silbermann
as I dab at the grease spattered
stove with the blue sponge
In what realms of past or future

lives were we related in what way
Are you diplomat   uncle   lover
and who am I
to tell you this?

The Past

He turned the modest car
onto the entrance ramp   accelerated
to match the speeding traffic
That morning she had clung to
his sleeve in the old way of fear
and desperation   He had not felt
it in a very long time   years
Today the boy would have been
twelve   A world away
it seemed he had never had
a son   or pain

The sun was caught in thin clouds
and forced to look into the water's flat
reflection   Willows dried their hair
along the harborside park   He cracked
open the car window   The highway
smelled of gasoline   oil burning

A willow suddenly burst
into innumerable splinters
Soundless explosions sprayed rock and water
into chrysanthemum patterns
A plane flew overhead   belly open
Trees and houses detonated in silence
their burning filling his throat
The couple in the next car
laughed and chatted   Traffic maintained
its dance of time and distance
He allowed the car to slow until
he found an exit.

Dixwell Sestina

Early in the year   the morning
not given to snow but cold
I nodded my head
to the radio's random music
not watching you change the tire
your car too close to the sidewalk

I studied cracks in the sidewalk
for clues that the morning
might yet unwind and tire
of its bad luck and cold
and the radio music
would drown out the ache in my head

I first noticed the bob of her head
like an old crow eying the sidewalk
She mocked a dance to my music
with her cane conducting the morning
She was hardly dressed for the cold
but curious about changing the tire

Just a shame you had to get a flat tire
she cackled   I could only nod my head
I seen ya settin out here in the cold
She scuffed slowly across the sidewalk
Well the Lord woke me up again this morning
She would tell the story   I lowered the music

I pray to Him to send me those angels' music
but He just like to see me tire
and goes and drags me up every morning
just the same   I got it in my head
I should be dead and carried down this sidewalk
and these old bones be all stiff and cold

18

I thought He'd be here last week I caught cold
but where's He – no angels   no music
same old cracks in the sidewalk
and your man over there changin a tire
She shuffled away shaking her head
Happy New Year to ya   Have a good mornin

You had finished with the tire
I shrugged   We smiled   You shook your head
She was so alive and it was morning.

Not My Dream

after the painting
The Head Hunter
by Arthur Heming

I am not Ojibwe
nor do I hunt for table meat
This is not my dream to tell

>Dancing lights had taken him
night after night into the realm
of ancestor warriors he had
dreamed would send moose
for winter food   moose
for wigwam hide   for moccasin
leather

>First arrow   then spear
had pierced the vital places
and he had tracked
blood through broken forest
keeping distance purposely until
the animal slowed   swayed and fell

>His brothers came to help
The village sang his feat
He tied the huge rack to his
back   With ancestor hunters
all around he bore it
to the white man's camp to sell

I am not Ojibwe
nor do I hunt for table meat
This is not my dream to tell

>Yet still I see
an angel span of antlers
wings him over snowbound trails
The beat of singing lights heralds

      his victory   The ancestors
    have blessed him well

But I am not Ojibwe
nor do I hunt for table meat
This is not my dream to tell.

Epilogue

After the
painting
Dejeuner en Provence
by Lucien Adams

He had agreed
to meet her in late
afternoon at the café not
far from her brother's
shop   He ordered
red wine and strawberries
perhaps expecting
a different conversation
So arrogant and fine he
had not been saddened
or angry but simply
removed himself as
one might leave a train
station without a word

while she remained
fastened to the chair by
regret and relief
fingering her napkin trying to
count the seeds on the surface of
the last strawberry.

Clothesline

After the watercolor
Washday—Rome
by Elizabeth Haigis

as the days repeated she

began to forget why

she had come to Rome

became distant from her

grief as simple acts

translated into exotic events

so that when they met

it seemed she had never been

married or widowed

so that when they loved

the air was made complete

their tenderness solid as earth

as the days repeated and

exotic events returned

to simple acts of keeping faith

cooking   washing up

odd that the sight of his laundry

hung out on her line

should cause her to

weep.

Second Wedding

They are sturdy children
tousled honey hair
ruddy cheeks
She is a shy three
He   six   defiant
I have always been good with children

It is fall   They play
outside   do not include me
I believe it is because of their mother
her sad illness and death
I am to marry
Nick   his blue eyes
good shoulders
his children

It will be a small wedding
My mother has made the cake
with the children's names   Nick's   mine
So the children will feel included

Nick's sister will wear black velvet
a high lace collar with rhinestones
I don't know what to wear
Wear blue   my mother crows
Doris says *Susan wore blue for
her second wedding*

The children eye me solemnly
I am a third sibling
Nick has been away two days
He has not called
The wedding is tonight.

Neighbors

After the painting
September Light
by Joan Hammeal

How many times
had he walked this path
in his near obsession
worn it bare himself in
what had become his custom
more ritual than habit
this distant visitation
of the light-filled house
wherein she breathed and
laughed and was
oblivious to her own
radiance   the lovely aura
for which he had yearned
until now these years
later it was enough
to watch the morning sun
caress the roof
that sheltered her.

Cathrine   My Sister

For all her love   Mother
shakes her head
reluctant to visit you
on what you'd hoped would be
your deathbed   We feel we cannot
desert you on your birthday
All the sisters and Mother will be
together this time at least
to celebrate your life?   Ours?
In a sun-filled hospital room
we share cake   present
our gifts to you
You are in forced high spirits
condescend to tease us
I have brought you tiger lilies
and snap dragons
They suit you so well   I say
You laugh   ask me to
bring out a box from the closet
For you on my birthday   you say
because you never liked it
In the box is your mink coat
I am speechless   touch
the sheen of dark fur
think I will never wear it
unless I am very cold.

Fast Kenny

New Britain Man Sought by Feds

In trouble more
than a few times   more
than his record showed
Then the robbery and shooting
interstate flight
armed and dangerous

Summer nights sometimes
all the kids played
kickball in the parking lot
between the long apartment
buildings in the project
teenagers running bases
for the little ones and parents
cheering from the back stoops
When captains chose teams
he would be among the first
chosen   even at age eight
Kenny ran faster than anyone.

Lansing NC 2014

I'm not saying I'd want to go back
The improvements sure brought a lot of jobs
constructing fine homes perched high in the woods
and bringing those artists and musicians
even poets to go on about the beauty of it all
I wouldn't go back to the poverty and worry
these mountain people knew
I just like to remember

I guess in this photo I was about 10—that's me
on the footbridge around 2014.
There was a row of shops
along Big Horse Creek Road
but not the artsy gift shops of today
There was a second hand store where
clothing was dumped in piles
the grocery   a pawn shop   a café
the motorcycle shop around the corner
some vacant store fronts and the new butcher shop
run by Ann Rose who farmed Rose Mountain
by herself—even butchered her own hogs
Across the street was the Volunteer Fire Dept
that burned one night   And just beyond that
a footbridge over the railroad tracks and the creek
leading to the town park
where gospel singers stood on
the bandstand and sang the old songs
of heavenly homes and the wages of sin.

About the Field

He was from the Department
of Agriculture   asking
was Grandpa going to harvest
the field   I explained
Grandpa was in Miami or Chicago
just living it up
but had not planted the field
for some years   had it hayed
once a summer for bedding
for Zausner's barn since ours was gone
and that contemporary built
next door on the old foundation

He said this was the only stop
he ever had to make in the area
the farm land all surrounded
with suburbs now   he was surprised
Grandpa didn't sell for building lots
or at least donate the field for a park

I told him most of the houses around
were built on our old land   I supposed
a park could be made around
Grandma's Uncle Rube and George Bartlett
the hired man who were buried
head to foot with brownstone markers

He didn't quite know what to do
with that   He left abruptly
but it was a good question
Grandma was buried in Fairview Cemetery
George and Rube were no kin
to Grandpa   Would he really want
to rest with them?

Photograph, June 1, 1928

They are posed on the front
porch of the Ridgewood down back
of Ortega at Indian Neck
No one seems glad to be
looking into the sun or
the camera   My grandfather
stands in his dress shirt and
bow tie holding his glasses
My grandmother sits with a cousin
on either side The sullen girl
on the end may be my mother
In front of her perhaps her sister
the pretty one who got a divorce
in the 1950's and grew
bitter and very heavy   We were
her only nieces and nephew but
she could never remember our names.

Picnic on the Hudson

after the painting
View of Cold Spring and
Mount Taurus
from Ft. Putnam
by Thomas Chambers

We would anticipate our Sunday
afternoons with near secrecy
hurry off after church as soon
as manners allowed
collect our basket from
the summer house and
hike a fair climb
to overlook the river
The Mighty Hudson
you would say and
I would laugh each time

Until the day the man
happened along the path
or had he followed?
a rough man not from town
leaning against his long rifle
asking weren't we afraid of bears
the question innocent enough
but how he never
took his eyes from me
while speaking with you
It made me squirm inside
my skin until you rested
your hand on mine
I looked him hard in the face
and he smirked and moved on

Now though you insist
he meant no harm
the place is spoiled for me.

In Confidence

After the painting known as
Untitled—Beach with Three Women
by Lucien Adams

By the time Mary and Patrice
arrived it was almost tea
She waited til they had eaten
their cress sandwiches and cakes to
suggest a stroll to watch the waves
gone wild with last night's storm
Their conversation idle stuff
of gardens   weather   parasols
She kept her tongue in check
until the pounding sea drowned out
their words for any
who might listen
told them both about the
gardener and his sly
advances how he had touched
her arm and watched her
move until she dared not
venture out alone for it seemed he
worked nearby no matter
where she walked   following
her with greedy eyes
And yet Papa
would think her foolish
she   too plain to rouse
the thoughts of any man
but surely Mary
would know what to do.

Sand Yachting

After the oil painting
After the Fog
by Marcelino Herrera Vegas

How perfectly adventurous
and modern speeding
along the beach
with the wind
filling the sail
Emmett manning the tiller
while Phoebe   Sara   and I
strove to sit proud
never showing a nerve
Emmett called us his
beautiful ballast
though in the end
gave it up to marry Phoebe
How fond and silly the memory
now when roadsters
travel at 50 miles per hour
and airplane travel
is not uncommon.

Lunchtime—West Haven

While three blocks inland
silent heat occupies
each particle   each thought
a lush breeze seduces
this stony shore

The cement pier shines
opal in the olive-green shimmer
of low tide   I follow to its end
my office clothing out of place

A bearded young man fishes
with two children
        a boy and a younger girl
the boy tells him where
in the tackle box to find extra hooks
I cannot guess at their relationship

Two dogs are chained
at opposite ends of a bench on which
two people sit   a man wearing
a cap inscribed
                SNET
    Building Div Safety Champs
                1981
He scratches the ears of the overweight
black dog looking dully out
over the Sound

A woman wearing shorts
reveals varicose veins streaming
down her thighs like rain
She feeds a handsome
brown and white spotted
hound from a thermos cup

The dog laps noisily
turns and laughs at me
with Kool-Aid red-stained mouth.

Propositioning Carrie Ann

After the watercolor
Making Plans
by Christine Drago

They had come aboard
with a six pack and shared
stories of the marina regulars

boats run aground by Sunday sailors
drunks boarding the wrong boat
waking up the wrong wife

Once they had hinted at
a fellow boater who had increased
his income substantially

accepting cargo at a designated
coordinate then dropping it close
to shore at high tide

Now they thought they knew him
well enough to bring him in
on this opportunity

They made it seem so natural
as if all friendships should evolve
to the point of illegal activity

He is listening with his poker face
dark glasses to hide any tell
as if actually considering

If they become too insistent
or possibly threatening he will
simply move on next tide

his only wish to get
them off the decks of
his true love Carrie Ann.

Summer Cottage

from the painting
Empty Chambers II
by Elizabeth Haigis

They had rented a house
on the point   with the sea
to one side and the bay
on the other   and now
it was September and the old
gardens ran amok with
blackberry canes hoarding
the waning sunlight
she was beginning to feel
the loss of this place
not hers to lose
as if the wealth of days
had been spent in currency
no longer minted

She had found a shell
(was it a whelk?) whole
intact upon the beach
and now she held it just
to feel its rippled sides.
Not knowing why
she whispered
into its vacant chamber
    I love you
    I love you
placed it on the window ledge
turning as he called

    OK. All packed up. You ready?

Where No Compass Guides

after a watercolor
Road Through Indiantown
by Mike Eagle

When he left home he knew
his way to where
the striper were running
in the channel off the wooden pier
big ones as the water warmed
They'd have a fine dinner
then   striper bathed in butter
He'd use mackerel for bait
his old reel   the one so easy
to his hand

But in the puddled parking lot
while clouds confuse a disenchanted
sky   bait and reel and fish forgotten
all he can do is stand
holding fast some line or painter
which?   until his old dog
patiently proceeds
to lead him home.

Home Visit

After the painting
High & Dry
by Donna Favreau

It seems like just a couple years

but Margie tells me it's six at least

because Morgan was only five last time

I came home   A drive around town reveals

she may be right

the tackle shop now a pizza joint

the drug store closed and vacant

boards on the town dock giving in

to splinters and rot

Rounding the bend down Old Cove

and there's Bart's sailboat in a cradle

by the garage and I remember now

hearing that he'd passed and how

he loved that thing like a woman

and I almost wish I could stay

move back and reclaim the old life

but then there was a reason

I moved on.

JOURNEY

Acrophobia II

Do not take me far
from this rock
earth
I need to belong to
the very clay
beneath layers of leaf and litter
beneath the matted roots

Do not entice me with
Ferris wheels
sight-seeing trips in single prop planes
flying horses
They are misplaced in me

I know best how to
cultivate the frozen ground
coax it to heave up
toward the nurturing moon
feed it with stones and sleet

to harvest from it
will
survival
other deeper passions.

Gestation

Time

move slow as wading

water birds

hunting spindle minnows

slower than

stars ascending

glaciers paring

earth's rock skin

move much slower than creation

let these old impatient passions die

my thighs   breasts   arms

reclaim myself

for this hour of birth

move slow as

I am midwife

mother

daughter

god.

Guilford Trilogy

I
West River
summer

Choose your steps along the meadow road
where anglers' trucks have left
their ruts and teens
conducting private experiments in
intimacy have driven their
borrowed cars   Follow
where deer cross into
the pine grove and skirt the second
field   Rocks and acorns trick
the feet down hill
where the river waits at once
placid and restless

Here are the stones of the old
mill   fallen to its memory
or still within its walls rising
massive on the far bank
No random boulders culled from
farmers' field   fixed with horsehair
in the mix   no
these stones quarried   cut   shaped
by promises of permanence
                            and yet
they serve now only to support
the shadows left by oak and beech
                by passing clouds and birds

Was the dooryard
here   close to where
the road ran down to ford
the stream   in summer nearly dry
the place quite plainly seen to end
in back yard swing sets   the grass
grown and mowed in the old road bed

and again what is the point of
endless speculation   these memories
were never mine nor those of anyone
I ever knew   What can be reconstructed
from the water's babbling?

II
Nut Plains
autumn

The root crops have been
taken up and brought
to light with eager hands
two-legged carrots   potatoes
with noses   Tattered vines hang
tangled in the trellis
the vibrant bushes beaten
to twigs in their rotting mulch
where over-ripe beans were
left to dry   hard and wizened
pods wait to be
gathered for seed

with marigold heads
and zinnia petals
let the cleome broadcast where
it will   I leave it to
itself   the wind   the turn
of plough blade

Among the snarl of brittle weed
and browning stalk   a luxury
of green   arugula and parsley
          as lime to the scurvied sailor
but I cannot bear to taste
or touch

Oh do not assume another
garden unless the earth
shall heave up stones
to prophesy and rocks cry out
the story   I am in
mourning for those days
of quiet disease   the sowing
                     growing

blessing not bestowed with
harvest but partaking
                             tomatoes
eaten warm with afternoon
hands   Oh do not
assume another
tomato laden splendor
from this brown decay
the sour stench of broccoli
past done   butternut squash
fouled with stinkbugs

The gloryless
heads of sunflowers hang devoured
by migrant birds.

III
Cockaponsett
winter

How shall I enter into
winter woods
Some preparation for extremes
double socks and boots
certainly the dog
The worn path lies soft and white
carpet for a bride
showing every step of the first
to sully its invitation   I have
been a thief of innocence
before   and now
I send the dog ahead   her
bold prints race and circle in
response to scents of mouse
and rabbit   coyote   deer
I track the ruined
newness leaving treads thick
as tires   Bare branches
buttress a sky heavy with omen
The gargoyle crows cast down
their calls of judgment

Blood warming with each stride
I acknowledge no set course but
random trails   The dog returns
with lolling mouth   darts off
when deer break cover   crash
through brush and briar
I inspect their bedding
ground   drink in the smell of
their startled fear   follow
where they fled through
narrow thoroughfares which I must
stoop to travel   Snow
flies sudden in all directions
With each step I forget

my name   The dog
has found her way
to warmth and food some place
I might have known once
But here is home   the den
dry and empty   I am
fat with summer's bounty though
no cub will share this winter's
sleep   I am too old
Were I to speak   what voice
would sound within
this holy tomb   I have
no words to offer to
glacial boulders   the root
side of earth   no words
for the frozen blessing covering
all and no desire for words

I am the ancient she bear
with grizzled snout and patchy
fur   claws worn and joints sore
I settle
into solstice
passionless   plain
and silent.

Lost Poem

It was not a poem
that would have been deemed
great   but I was fond
of its sentiment   the picture
it created of the growing
garden   the awareness
of resources   the birds
those sweet sparrows
caught in the moment
of that poem I have lost
no landscape of cosmic
proportions or icon
of literary paradigm
but a simple snapshot
a moment of joy
well captured.

Garden Journal—July 3

(Lost Poem—Found)

A garden is
a tenuous thing   dependent
upon factors over which
I have no control
and yet responsive to my
careful tending
Today I staked
tomato plants grown
lush and wild already
showing hard green
globes the size of golf balls
I turn water
on the squash plants
started late again this year but
coming on   Tomorrow
I will set drip hoses
for more efficient watering
but for this
hot afternoon I leave
the sprinkler on   watch
sparrows flutter in
and out   splashing
like naughty children.

Anger

The cat has scarred
the window casing   shameless
sleeps beneath her mark

All night my wrists and forearms
ache   my hands work at themselves
I am orphaned   turn to dreams
whose plots unfold and thicken

I am caught in a timeless place
a surfeit of sun
where trees fatten with
leaves they have worn before
and birds repeat their senseless calls
songs falling to my ears
like overripe plums split
at the skins   the pulp
exposed and I consume
the jellied fruit to become
what that reality demands

The cat awakes to gnash her teeth
at the window
The mourning doves
the placid doves
patiently pick at old seed.

Awake

Cricket

under my skull or

clinging to the window screen

vibrating the cross wires

against each other

amplifying

a street light patch

on the closet door

to movie screen proportions

playing reels of memories

and rerun might-have-beens

until the tarnished stars

fade.

Exile

The land is such that no bird
sings   Sparrows worry their language
of bushes and beetles
warn lest crows snatch
hatchlings from the nest

They do   A large crow pecks
at what scant morsel clings to
tiny bones   violence in the back
yard   At least
in forest fen they take
their meals in private dining
Here   there is no pretense

It is just this
no morning mist
to burn from shambling hills
or skipping stream
no heron stately stalks
no egret starts up flying
white against the blue
no wren warbles to
green scents of day
no wood thrush haunts this
dusk with lullaby

No little chance has brought
a mockingbird to sing
into this wilderness
a borrowed hope.

Talisman

Gray granite pocked
and swirled with rusty
iron this rock is
chosen from its stream
bed as a directional rune
a point of reference for
I am a stranger within
my self   The purposes
defining my life crumble
washed away in
a stream of days and events
beyond me   I am
not fulfilled in them
nor do I fulfill

Become as silence
the stone says   stilled
from doing   thinking   feeling

This dying is
slow   in bits
of being until
only the rock remains
the map without a key
the way without a path
the fact without comment
or commitment

Choose any point from
which to start   any direction
to travel into light
It's all the same
The map is silent
The rock remains.

On The Footbridge

After the oil painting
West Cornwall, Connecticut
by David Johnson

those beastly August days the sky

a blank disc white and void

oppressing all creation

for reasons she could not understand

she would go out at noon

at the height of intensity to walk

into the woods but not for the shade

or the whisper of pine needles

dropping in the heat   not for

birds simply stuck to their branches

or deer too hot to startle

nor for the relief of solitude but

to emerge from that welcome gloom

to stand on the footbridge over

the sullen stream

now slowed to a trickle

stand suspended between

those red clay banks

searching for what

she could not name.

Challenge

What flagrant storm has riled
this southern sea where white foam
crests the jade green waves that
      roll and break
      roll and break
their hiss and pound diminished
only by the wind engaging sea grass
in some reckless tarantella
in footlights of the dying day

while I who came for solace
ache for some answer to a call to
risk my comfort for the dreams of youth

weigh out what yet is possible to one
whose prime is past.

Impetus

I feel sure
that other poems lie
about in those dusty
corners waiting to be
hauled out from hiding
wiped clean the
best ones polished bright
and sent off to be
appraised

For now it seems
I walk in narrow aisles
a hoarder within
the clutter of
life prescribed
like bitter medicine or
the book of Ecclesiastes
a time for this
a time for that
each time spelled out
in obligation

Tell me not
how others rise before
the rosy-fingered dawn to
ply their words upon
the page. For me
the previous day's not done

Forget the clock
the hours that measure
Give me passionate
sirens in the night or
wind chimes jingling
in the garden

For poetry I need
an open path   a waiting
sky   and air uncluttered
by resolve.

Nearing the Solstice

Low in the sky the sun casts

its amber light on phragmites

and the southwestern side of trees

Day is short

hours run out before their time

I am left pulling at threads of expectation

still to be realized

that other life

where I am the Grandma Moses of

words and images I dare not dream

until

the earth turns in its season

light is reborn

a clearer vision calls.

Listening for Orion

We have grown
unaccustomed to stars
Between city and suburb
they keep shy council
whispering vaguely
to high passing jets

but here
withstanding the occasional
house light I almost
hear them

I would go where
wild air bears them up
above the mountainsides
to be deafened by their
strident chorus.

Reserve America

We will explore the eastern slopes
of the Appalachians by
automobile
motorcar
Dodge Caravan precisely
wherever the road leads
except for the necessity
of having a destination
for the night
random camping
being frowned upon most places
reservations are required
and so I plot
a route by MapQuest
and locate campgrounds within
an X mile radius of
some city en route
researching each accommodation
for the availability of hot showers
until exhausted with planning
I present an itinerary
to my traveling companion
who complains
we have been there before or
seen that already as if
campgrounds grow on trees.

Love After All

An unsuspecting swan trails

shining threads within its sapphire wake

A vivid branch flares red among

the dowdy leaves of late summer

Salt scent of turning tide

teases my soul to far off

places where you are as if

thirty years were some swift

accident of good fortune that

you should love me after

all this time.

Unpacking the Move

I seem to have moved

between galaxies instead

of 600 miles southwest

and now must reconsider

each item wrapped in tissue

to see where it will fit

into this unfamiliar place

so beautiful I dreamed it

once when I was lost.

Learning the House

Well-kept for ninety-one
updated yet still charming
gleaming floors a bit uneven
tall windows wavy-paned

I have learned the light
switches for each room
the way the sun sparks the
pin oak at 4:00   where
the baking pans were put away
the way the air moves through
the hall between front door and back

I am unprepared
for the quiet of brick
more used to the creaks and
sighs of old wood yielding
to age and weather

No   this house stands staid   holding
the almost whir of fan blades
absorbing music of crickets
and katydids and didnts

The fierce stars answer
with their own
peculiar song.

Veranda Lullaby

Sky fades to dusty purple
Cicadas drone a rasping rattle
The hound barks at deer
unseen behind the scrim of trees
Hummingbirds vie for a turn
at the feeder   chasing
and chattering

I seek no omen
no harbinger of good or ill
save fireflies
dancing for each other
I sit in the shelter of
the veranda that wraps
its arms around this house
and it is enough.

SPIRIT

Creation

When all was ready   poised
at the edge   not of chaos
which must contain the seeds
of order   when all was
ready   poised
at the edge of nothing
a something God shouted
GO
and all that
was ever to be something
pelted into nothing
to become

And the nothing became
chaos   and all became
seed

all particles   atoms and molecules
elements of gas and metal
each to form and reform order
in myriad destinies as
fragile as a blink or stable
as forever.

A Priming of Parts

Once running
the operation of this
machine is
simple
its motor parts and
controls are
programmed to perform
automatically
almost spontaneously

When there is need to
change to manual control
slow the responses
        reprogram
or change the dye completely
         shut down
         retool

it is the restarting
that is difficult
What generation   line voltage
what chemical
      catalyst
         heat   light
what ritual
what sacrifice.

Drum Song

                    for Soon and the Tea Group

We part to take
other roads to the same
place   You give me
a drum from Africa
I do not know
its history   maker   design
symbolic purpose   except
to keep time   to measure a space
between beats   to count into
the future

Shall we believe its pulse
to be certainty   We strike
and it answers us   or anyone
shows no partiality   an object
of trust somehow   to be
used in the calling
out of sisters in faith

And if my heart should break
along the way   I shall beat
my drum to keep
the time we are together
within the heart of God.

Because…

Isaiah 58:6

I have been called
to witness the grief that fills
the days of others
the pain of aging bodies
the accidents of flesh and blood
the anguish and hope within
the failing breath of any given day

Because I have shared time
with tears and tales
of twisted lives entangled
with destruction   or minds deceived
by persecutions real
or fabricated by delusion

Because I have been wooed
by artists of the scam
still holding to some tattered ideology
that what they do is just

Because this is the fast that I choose
Because these woes so tightly woven
become my way and shelter
I am dry bones   a faded page
my own truth deep as marrow
my yearning constant as dust.

Parable

Today she is burdened
with visions   unbidden
some sorcery has raised them
from dust blown across
      the street
      the yard of a madwoman
      the bed of a stream run dry

   An infant is blessed
       as was the Buddha
   with the knowledge of speech
       hears what the pines tell
       the wind to carry away
       hears the serpent's long plan
       of revenge
   and says only
       Mother   I am hungry

   A young woman holds to the hand
   of her betrothed   her love
   for another burning her fingers
   the falsehood tearing her sleeve
   where their coats touch   even
   that touch a deceit
       How can I tell him

   A young man has thrown away
   his desire   his past and future
       anything that might have
       claimed him
He hangs by his belt in a cell
He absently squeezes the hand-warmed metal
He lies down to sleep in the railroad bed
He speaks to no one

She will take these burdens
to the river's edge   caress each
as one might steady a nervous horse
and leave them for the deeper water
to bear.

Burial Rites

The paper was colorful
white on one side and gaily striped on the other
We folded the square into nine sections
and in the center placed our tokens:
sugar for sweetness
rue because this death was regrettable
rosemary for remembrance
thyme because there was no more
a pink cleome for celebration
peanut husks for the body just a shell
yellow rose petals for friendship
popcorn kernels for surprises
chocolate bits to make it better
snowflakes for his passion
stars to guide the way
olive oil enough for a feast
sweet oil for anointing
dust to which we all must return
the sign of the cross for forgiveness
This we folded up and tied with twine

We made a small fire in the yard
and when there were coals enough
placed the packet there to burn
turning our backs
hoping for healing
standing in silence
with our tears and
no other way to
say goodbye.

Bereaved

for Totsie Bruce

Overnight a sudden arctic rush

sent ground plants

hurrying to wither and leaves

drop down before they could

change color

Tomorrow we will huddle

at the family plot to bury your ashes

you for whom death was

a reprieve.

Snow will come

Predictions cast no doubt
The moon of early evening shrouds
herself in hoary cloud and I
am left uneasy with details
left undone as if the fact
of snow could silence
all as easily as
some sweet apocalypse
to make common all
disparities of circumstance
sifting mercy or disguised
by a forgiveness so deep
not one might escape the peace
that falls so gently
so relentlessly when the
snow will come.

Love Song

Within this world   my home
for this time when I must endure
separation from my Love
I love the love of flesh and bone
the strength with which my love desires
sweetness of my children's tears
grace of beasts made dumb by grace
the dank earth's power to beget
tree and fruit   leaf and flower

Within this world I love the sky of morning
blue or gray   shadows long with afternoon
a winter slap of cold across my face
these things almost suffice for here and yet
given their blessed imperfections serve
as markers for my one true Love
a Love demanding none of this but all
of Love   the One in whom my restless
heart may rock and rest.

Advent

*Where do we go
from here*   she asks
her hold on life so
tenuous   When we met
she was intrigued by the T
and would consider how long
before the train would reach
beneath the bridge in case
she felt the need to jump
Each week I drove to Boston
wondering
would she have made it
to one life or the next
Not your normal suicide case
she does not belong here
but only wants to live with Jesus

It is the time of waiting
Advent   like a pregnancy
the time of preparation
Where do we go   she asks
I wonder how we get
to the place of expectation
that some fragile child
two thousand years old
should call us to some meaning
beyond what we can scrape together
with pretty words and anthems
meant to bless   Where
do we go for faith against the bitter wind

and yet above the streetlights' glare
one star.

In Surrender

After the sculpture
Winter
by Mary Knollenberg

What is the place

where prayer begins

the hope that time is

more than day upon day

more than the tedium

of waking and sleeping

expansion and contraction

elasticity of hours

lost in concentration

gained in conversation

The dawn blooms

the sunset fades

the mystery of stars

swirls on and on

Is it finally in humility

we arrive at supplication

having seen we are

so small

so small

A Winter's Tale

Let's say Mary was 14
and pregnant   traveling
with her fiancé   He could be 19 or so
He is not the father
Let's say it was winter   but not
like New England or anyplace
really cold   more like South Carolina or
northern Florida   cool evenings
cooler nights
Let's say she had her first
contractions in the late evening
and they didn't have
anywhere to go
Let's say they were far from town
or maybe they were just plain scared
when they hid in a barn
and he helped her birth the child
a beautiful little boy
a cosmic child with eyes wide open
Let's say a shepherd opened
the barn in the morning to let out
the sheep   and found them
all three sleeping in the hay
and he didn't call the sheriff
but his grandmother   his wife   his children
his good neighbor folks and
they came bringing what gifts they had
baby clothes handed down
a little rattle   a warm blanket
Let's say the grandmother washed
the baby   and the mother
and found them fit and healthy

Let's say the shepherd let them take
the back bedroom for just a while
and the neighbors dropped by
with casseroles and a ham
and an old spinster gave the child
her father's gold watch
and the grandmother gave Mary
some herbs to help with her milk
and they brought the child
to church next Sunday
and received a blessing there
Let's say they just packed up
and left one night with thanks
but no forwarding address
or explanation
Let's say that folks remembered them
for years and years and wondered
what ever became of that little family.

Toward Epiphany

The gift paper is returned
to its accustomed place
the bows in another box
to keep them crisp
Décor washed or dusted
wrapped in left-over tissue
Greeting cards reread
kept for reply
discarded
the best saved for collage

I am left a wandering mage
still traveling an Advent season
without camel or donkey
my companion this old dog
A full moon barely separates
night from day
the path is bright
no excuse

Still seeking I
have lost the way
Perhaps he lies beside
a wilder road.

Mandala

It is said that
the largest living entity is
an aspen grove in Colorado
The aspen trees are
all connected at their roots
so that they become one
system   a breathing   organic whole

I say that
the largest spiritual entity is
the Holy Spirit indwelling God's people
in every place and time
connected at their hearts
so that they become one
Spirit   a mystic cosmic whole

And I say that
Spirit seeks us   calls us   moves us
to enter a great circle
a dance and swirl of faith and not faith
of belief and unbelief
a spiral leading down and up
all at once.

In the Woods   God

In the woods   God
is clearly seen in
silver birch   swollen stream
and blue winged teal
strident sunsets
early morning dew making
crystal of the conifer
branches and always through
the calling night of
coyote song and
tremulous owls   The stars
shine out in multiples
and Milky Ways   the dusty
prints of God's least sandal

Why then am I
surprised to see
stars of mica
in the tarry black roadway
shining in mid-afternoon?

Fifteen minutes

Fifteen minutes from road
to cove over well-worn paths through
tangles of Eastern woodland
brush and briar and slender birch with
full grown maple and oak   a few
small stands of pine and
squirrels scuffling about
everywhere teasing the dog

My body wants to stride out
quickly cover ground but these
few acres soon are spent
I come empty to the rock overlooking
marsh   gulls   boats the
light-bearing water so
inaccessible

My heart says linger while
afternoon sun plays upon
those golden leaves dancing
in cerulean space those wisps
of cloud shifting
scents of autumn's sweet
decay   burst pods spilling
seeds of next year's growth

Linger   let
time be fluid in you
Drink in the divine.

Thanksgiving

From geese who mount the cobalt sky
and in their fine formation fly
to deer who leap through lingering maize
Each creature has its way to praise

Yet we for all our lust for life
are mired in struggle woe and strife
unless we rise and dare confess
to some brief prayer of thankfulness

though many still tend to deny
the bent of the Divine to bless.

Swallowed by Sinkhole

> As Eli Raz peered into a hole
> in the Dead Sea shore,
> the earth opened up and swallowed him.
> AP—6/23/09

The Dead Sea is the lowest point
on earth   One might think one could
not get any lower   could not fall
beneath its the salty terra firma shore
but this is holy land   Odd
things have happened here and will
again if all those crazy prophets have
their way   It was Eli raised young Samuel
to be one of Israel's finest   though his own
sons disappointed   It was David peered into the cave
to see Saul taking a dump   It was Jonah swallowed
by a great fish on his way to avoid God

Be careful what you swallow
when you read of this   You may become
convinced that slavery is just
that love expressed is forbidden
that women should not speak out   Or worse
you may use reason to disregard the truth
that moved a desert people to value
compassion and mercy   though who
can claim to keep that narrow path

Translated rightly they learned not
to murder   not to make their living
by theft   not to abandon their feeble
parents too old to support
themselves   The rules were not what we think
we know or live out and yet
compassion and mercy remain
entwined in our desire to be whole

What was our latter day Eli
thinking beneath the earth   The report
says that he is a geologist that
he wrote his will on a postcard
He was rescued and now
maps areas tending toward collapse.

Lazarus   Afterward

I lay deep in death
my body slowly returning
to the dust of stars
my soul not far
from my sisters' love
held fast in the knowledge of God
until called into focus
by an undeniable command
Come out
rematerialized and released
trailing my winding sheet
I follow

To what end?
Shall my former life remain
unchanged? I suffer
death threats from those
who would discredit
this reawakening
My sisters hover
tentative and uncertain
My days seem purposeless
except that through me
God has been glorified.

Legion

and he shouted at the top of his voice, What have you to do with me, Jesus, Son of the Most High God? I adjure you by God, do not torment me... My name is Legion, for we are many.
Mark 5:7-9

We like the hills
for sleep   where the sun
falls first and last
to redden sleepers' eyes awake
Tombs are best
for we are not alone   The earth
is tender there   the stones
seem not to gouge
the face or stick
the softest parts

We like the crannies
for lament   when we are overcome
and hide among the rocks to howl
we are alone
we are afraid
we are alone
and we are many
We are the sum of all
our ancestors in one   We hold
their memories with all
they have forgotten   We hear
their voices calm
and shrill   We are
their grave   the bearers
of their hope   their childhood
dreams   their passions
furious or sweet
their bones   the way
their flesh was formed or filled
We are their anthem
and their slave   We are

their children
Set me free
but do not let them die
Jesus of Nazareth.

The Mathematics of Grapes

We cast discerning eyes
on microcosmic events
and hope to find some
explanation for whatever it is
that is going on   We dare not
consider the lilies or the mustard
seeds lest we are assigned
labels by those who do not
share our world perspective
Equations exist to show the fiddlehead
unfurl   the frond full grown   Shorelines
are duplicated every sixth iteration
proven in maps shot from satellites
beyond the atmosphere that gives
us breath   We know how yeast works
to make bread rise   tell me then
what is the ratio of love to vines
the mathematics of grapes?

Waning Moon at Break of Day

A fading pearl

in a still-gray sky

rests almost round

on silver maple boughs

then slips slowly down

to the mountains' blue

a mystery

too profound for explanation.

Acknowledgements

Fifteen Minutes was previously published in the Guilford Poets Guild Tenth Anniversary Anthology;

Veranda Lullaby and Learning the House were previously published in Our Changing Environment, Guilford Poets Guild 20th Anniversary Anthology.

Karen Gronback Johnson has been writing poetry from an early age. She has been a member of the Guilford Poets Guild in Guilford, CT, since 1978. Karen and her husband, Michael, retired to Virginia four years ago, and she is now privileged to work with the Ridgeline Writers. She writes poetry to describe the journey of her living, and hopefully resonates with others' journey, as well.

Karen Johnson's collection of poems summon the full range of what makes poetry a kind of ladder to the stars. The beauty of sparkling language; the narratives of small and large dramas; the keen and lovely observation of flights of the spirit that are yet tethered to daily life in a concrete world -- all this, and more, suffuse her poems. Full of reckonings with time, memory, loss, exultation, God, the poems shine like the inner dome of heaven. Reading poem after poem, we find ourselves on a kind of pilgrimage into eternity. Grounded in place, and in her remarkably varied life, Johnson's poems fuse language and poetic form with subjects so large -- death, justice, the far horizons of the human soul -- that the poems seem unbounded, limitless. Yet they are life as one so attentive as Karen Johnson experiences life daily. This is our life, her poems say, very quietly. This is our existence, under heaven.

Frank Levering - Author, Poet, Playwright

The poems in Karen Johnson's *Story, Journey, Spirit* are deeply complex and varied. They offer the delights of her love for the elements and spirit of the natural world; her talent for description and rich, often surprising imagery; her gifts for storytelling, humor and irony; and the originality of her perspective on all things worldly and beyond. The complexity of her material is managed perfectly by its clean expression and presentation, with artful lineage and spacing replacing punctuation. For me, the poem Love Song sums up and exemplifies this extraordinary combination. But you should read every poem. Twice.

Nancy Fitz-Hugh Meneely
Author, *Letter from Italy, 1944*

Never much of a devote´ of poetry, that all changed for me with reading and hearing Karen Johnson read from her collections of wise, humorous, sensuous poems. Ms. Johnson's miniature works of art have made me a colossal fan of her work and the genre.

Richard Rouse Author, *The Welcome Home Door,*
Tales of Appalachia and Beyond

www.ingramcontent.com/pod-product-compliance
Lightning Source LLC
Chambersburg PA
CBHW071156090426
42736CB00012B/2348